True Statements from the 66

Dr. Bernard Kent, Jr.

All biblical quotations are from the New King James version.

Cover Design: Dr. Bernard Kent, Jr.

Published by G Publishing LLC

ISBN: 979-8-9894404-4-3

Printed in the United States of America

Acknowledgments

Two people that are important and loved by me are my Godson and Goddaughter

This book is dedicated to Raymond Newton, who simply calls me "Doc." Ray, you are special, a torch of light that is evident in your love. You never forget or be too busy to come by or call often to make sure all is well with me. Sweet, lovable, caring all smiles when you say "God daddy" I love you.

Trey Kelly Burrison is a tank of love with a great smile that expresses care all the time. When you call to check and see how I am doing makes me feel like a King without a crown.

Godchildren can be sweet and an important part of the family. Ray and Trey are family, and an example of what Godchildren should be toward Godparents. Thanks, and may you continue to be sweet and lovable. Both of you will always be in my heart. Thanks, guys love you much.

God Daddy

Thanks to my son Al for the time and effort he put forth to complete this work. Much love son.

Table of Contents

Introduction

When reading the statements in this book, only select the true answers. In each section, a single or multiple answer may be true. After making a choice, all correct answers are given in the answer section. Scripture is given with the chapter and verse for each answer. No statement is provided for false answers.

Information was obtained from each of the sixty-six and incorporated as True-False statements.

The author desires that as you read through this book, a greater appreciation will develop for truth. Often what is seen to be true can be misleading and invalid. Reading the sixty-six books will increase knowledge of what is in the sixty-six.

There are sixty-six books in the Bible which equals thirty-nine in the Old Testament and twenty-seven in the New Testament.

The New King James Bible served as a platform for the recorded statements in this book. Other versions may be read for better understanding. And now "True Statements from the 66."

Old Testament

1. Genesis
    A. Genesis is believed to be written by Moses.
    B. Genesis was written by Abraham.
    C. Genesis is a book of the Pentateuch.
    D. Jacob lived in the land of Midian.
    E. A and C
    F. B and D

2. Exodus
    A. Moses and Joshua were brothers.
    B. The plague of the firstborn was upon Israel.
    C. Moses and Aaron were brothers.
    D. The slaves in Egypt made bricks out of grass.

3. Leviticus
    A. A grain offering was a sack of potatoes.
    B. A fellowship offering could only be a female animal.
    C. A male animal without defects was offered as a burnt offering before the Lord.
    D. A weasel was deemed clean and eaten by the Israelites.

4. Numbers
   A. Daniel is the author of Numbers.
   B. Numbers is not a book of the
      Pentateuch.
   C. The Passover was a time of rebellion.
   D. A Nazarite abstained from wine and
      other fermented drinks.

5. Deuteronomy
   A. Deuteronomy is not a book of the
      Pentateuch.
   B. Moses was buried by Saul.
   C. One's life could be saved if he
      entered a City of Refuge.
   D. The people in Israel never went to
      war.

6. Joshua
   A. The people marched around Jericho
      nine times.
   B. The people of Canaan always
      defeated the Israelites.
   C. Joshua replaced Aaron as the leader
      of Israel.
   D. The people marched around Jericho
      seven times and the walls collapsed.

7. Judges
   A. Deborah was not a judge in Judges.
   B. Samson killed a thousand men with the jawbone of a donkey.
   C. Everyone did as he saw fit.
   D. Samson's strength left him after his hair was shaved.

8. Ruth
   A. Ruth was an Israelite.
   B. Ruth had two daughters in law.
   C. "Where you go, I will go" was said by Ruth.
   D. Boaz married Ruth.

9. I Samuel
   A. Samuel was a prophet of the Lord.
   B. King Saul was not anointed by Samuel.
   C. Samuel ministered to the Lord under Eli.

10. II Samuel
   A. David had two wives when he went to Hebron.
   B. Davis was condemned by Samuel for his sin with Bathsheba.
   C. Amnon was not related to Tamar when he raped her.
   D. Absalom killed Amnon for raping his daughter Tamar.

11. I Kings
    A. Nathan was not a prophet of Israel.
    B. Solomon was not a king of Israel.
    C. Davis was Solomon's son.
    D. Nathan was a prophet of Israel.

12. II Kings
    A. Naaman was healed of leprosy.
    B. Elijah was taken up to heaven in a
       whirlwind.
    C. Amaziah was King of Israel for
       twenty-nine years.
    D. Elisha was called bald by some
       youth.

13. I Chronicles
    A. Davis was allowed to build a temple
       to the Lord.
    B. 6,800 men joined David at Hebron
       for battle.
    C. One of Caleb's sons was Ira.
    D. King Hiram built a temple for the
       Lord.

14. II Chronicles
    A. Uzziah was sixteen when he became
       king in Jerusalem.
    B. Josiah was eight when he became
       king in Jerusalem.
    C. The queen of Sheba gave Solomon
       great wealth.
    D. Solomon asked the Lord for wisdom.

15. Ezra
   A. Ezra received permission from King
      Artaxerxes to build a temple in
      Jerusalem.
   B. Zerubbabel built an altar to sacrifice
      burnt offerings to the Lord.
   C. King Cyrus was given all the
      kingdom of the earth.

16. Nehemiah
   A. Nehemiah was a cupbearer to King
      Artaxerxes.
   B. Sanballat ridiculed the Jews for
      rebuilding the walls of Jerusalem.
   C. The walls of Jerusalem were rebuilt
      with no breaks in it.

17. Esther
   A. A woman had to complete twelve
      months of beauty treatments, six
      months of oil and myrrh, and six
      months of perfume and cosmetics
      before appearing before the King
      Ahasuerus.
   B. Mordecai adopted Esther.
   C. Haman was hanged on a gallows he
      made for Mordecai.

18. Job
   A. All of Job's children were killed by a
      wind.
   B. Job accepted his suffering with joy.

C. Job's three friends were Eliphaz,
Bildad, and Zophar.

19. Psalms
A. Psalm 100 is a chapter of sorrow.
B. Psalm 31 does not provide refuge in
the Lord.
C. Moses is believed to have written
Psalms.
D. There are five books in the book of
Psalms.

20. Proverbs
A. One should trust in the Lord and not
depend on his understanding.
B. Solomon wrote the tenth chapter of
Proverbs.
C. A good name is more desirable than
riches.
D. One should get wisdom and
understanding.

21. Ecclesiastes
A. There is a time for everything.
B. Remember the creator while a youth.
C. Do not be quick to speak.
D. A good name is better than fine
perfume.
E. Do not delay in fulfilling a vow.

22. Song of Solomon
A. The Song of Solomon is not about
love.

B. Beauty is expressed in the Song of Solomon.

C. Love is not an element in the Song of Solomon.

D. The Song of Solomon is a book of romantic poetry.

23. Isaiah

A. The wicked should forsake his ways.

B. The birthday of Jesus is not given in chapter nine.

C. Isaiah saw the Lord at the death of King Uzziah.

D. Hezekiah's life was extended fifteen years after being told he would die.

24. Jeremiah

A. The Lord knew Jeremiah before he was born.

B. Jeremiah was not a prophet of God.

C. Jeremiah was not allowed to get married.

25. Lamentation

A. The Lord's throne does not reign forever, and His throne does not endure forever.

B. In chapter one, verses one through twenty-two, Jerusalem faced destruction.

C. A plea for God's mercy is given in chapter five.

   D. The Lord's mercy is good to those whose hope is in Him and who seek Him.

26. Ezekiel
    A. Four judgments were set against Jerusalem.
    B. Ezekiel was a watchman for Israel.
    C. Ezekiel was a priest.
    D. The valley of dry bones is given in Chapter 37.

27. Daniel
    A. Nebuchadnezzar ordered the fire in the furnace to be seventy times seventy hotter than the Hebrew boy.
    B. Shadrack, Meshack, and Abednego were thrown into a furnace.
    C. Another name given to Daniel was Belteshazzar.

28. Hosea
    A. Hosea did not show love to his wife.
    B. Three children of Hosea were Jerrell, Loruhmah, and Lo-Ammi.
    C. Israel burned incense and sacrifice to Baal.
    D. Hosea was married to Gomer, and an adulterous wife.

29. Joel
    A. Old men will dream dreams, and young
       men will see vision.
    B. Jerusalem will never be invaded by
       foreigners.
    C. The moon will be turned to blood.

30. Amos
    A. Harm will not come to those complacent
       in Zion.
    B. A man may flee from a lion only to run
       into a bear.
    C. All sinners will die by the sword of
       Sampson.
    D. Three chapters begin with the word
       "hear."

31. Obadiah
    A. The Lord will destroy the wise men of
       Edom.
    B. You should not look down on your
       brother.
    C. Obadiah contains three chapters.

32. Jonah
    A. Jonah ran away from the Lord and
       never went to Nineveh.
    B. Jonah was in the belly of a fish for three
       days and nights.
    C. After the Lord spoke to Jonah a second
       time, he went to Nineveh.

33. Micah
    A. God's judgment was against Samaria.
    B. Israel will crush grapes and not drink
        the wine.
    C. Israel misery = Do not trust a neighbor
        and do not put confidence in a friend.

34. Nahum
    A. The Lord will not leave the guilty
        unpunished.
    B. Nineveh enslaved nations by
        prostitution.
    C. Locusts do not strip the land.
    D. The Lord is good and a refuge in times
        of trouble.

35. Habakkuk
    A. The righteous will live by his work.
    B. The righteous will live by his faith.
    C. The Sovereign Lord is my strength.
    D. Habakkuk stands in awe of the Lord.
    E. Woe to him who piles up stolen goods.

36. Zephaniah
    A. Assyria was destroyed and Nineveh
        was desolate.
    B. Cush was not slain by the sword.
    C. Zephaniah served under the reign of
        Solomon.
    D. Zephaniah was the son of Cushi.

37. Haggai
    A. Haggai was not a messenger of the
       Lord.
    B. The word of the Lord came to Haggai to
       speak to Zerubbabel.
    C. Haggai served under King David.
    D. Haggai was a priest under Daniel.

38. Zechariah
    A. Five horns scattered Jerusalem, Judea,
       and Israel.
    B. The nations that fought against
       Jerusalem, their flesh will not.
    C. It is the Lord who makes the storm
       cloud.

39. Malachi
    A. Esau was Jacob's brother.
    B. "I hate divorce," says the Lord.
    C. One can rob God with tithes and
       offerings.
    D. The lips of a priest should preserve
       knowledge.
    E. God's name will be great from the rising
       to the setting of the sun.

Answers 1-39

1. Genesis
   A — True - The first book of Moses.
   C — True - The first five books of the Bible are the Pentateuch.

2. Exodus
   A — Exodus 4:14

3. Leviticus
   C — Leviticus 1:3

4. Numbers
   D — Numbers 6: 1

5. Deuteronomy
   C — Deuteronomy 4:42

6. Joshua
   D — Joshua 5:4

7. Judges
   C — Judges 17:5
   D — Judges 16:18-19

8. Ruth
   C — Ruth 1:16
   D — Ruth 4:13

9. I Samuel
   A — I Samuel 4:20
   C — I Samuel 1:20 and I Samuel 2:11

10. II Samuel
    A — II Samuel 2:2

11. I Kings
    A — I Kings 1:32

12. II Kings
    A — II Kings 4:14
    B — II Kings 2:1
    C — II Kings 14:2
    D — II Kings 2:23

13. I Chronicles
    B — I Chronicles 12:23-24
    C — I Chronicles 4:15

14. II Chronicles
    A — II Chronicles 26:1
    B — II Chronicles 24:1
    C — II Chronicles 9:8-9
    D — II Chronicles 1:10

15. Ezra
    B — Ezra 3:2
    C — Ezra 1:2

16. Nehemiah
    A — Nehemiah 1:11
    B — Nehemiah 4:1-2
    C — Nehemiah 6:1

17. Esther
    A — Esther 2:12
    B — Esther 2:15
    C — Esther 7:10

18. Job
    A — Job 1:9
    C — Job 5:11

19. Psalms
    D — Psalms 1, Psalms 42, Psalms 73,
    Psalms 90, and Psalms 107

20. Proverbs
    A — Proverbs 3:5
    B — Proverbs 10:1
    C — Proverbs 22:1
    D — Proverbs 4:5

21. Ecclesiastes
    A — Ecclesiastes 3:1
    B — Ecclesiastes 12:1
    C — Ecclesiastes 5:2
    D — Ecclesiastes 7:1
    E — Ecclesiastes 5:4

22. Song of Solomon
    B — Song of Solomon 4:1
    D — True

23. Isaiah
    A — Isaiah 55:7
    C — Isaiah 6:1
    D — Isaiah 38:5

24. Jeremiah
    A — Jeremiah 1:4-5
    C — Jeremiah 16:1

25. Lamentation
    B — Lamentation 1:21
    C — Lamentation 5:1-22
    D — Lamentation 3:25

26. Ezekiel
    A — Ezekiel 14:21
    B — Ezekiel 3:17
    C — Ezekiel 1:3
    D — Ezekiel 37

27. Daniel
    B — Daniel 3:26
    C — Daniel 1:7

28. Hosea
    B — Hosea 1:4-9
    C — Hosea 11:2
    D — Hosea 1:2

29. Joel
    A — Joel 2:28
    B — Joel 3:17
    C — Joel 2:31

30. Amos
    B — Amos 5:19
    D — Amos 3:1, Amos 4:1, Amos 5:1

31. Obadiah
    B — Obadiah 1:12
    C — Obadiah 1

32. Jonah
    B — Jonah 1:17

C — Jonah 3:1-2

33. Micah
    A — Micah 1:3
    B — Micah 6:4
    C — Micah 7:7

34. Nahum
    A — Nahum 1:3
    B — Nahum 3:4
    D — Nahum 1:7

35. Habakkuk
    B — Habakkuk 3:19
    C — Habakkuk 3:2
    D — Habakkuk 2:6

36. Zephaniah
    A — Zephaniah 2:13
    D — Zephaniah 1:11

37. Haggai
    B — Haggai 2:20-21

38. Zechariah
    B — Zechariah 14:12
    C — Zechariah 10:1

39. Malachi
    A — Malachi 1:2
    B — Malachi 2:16
    C — Malachi 3:8-9
    D — Malachi 2:7
    E — Malachi 1:11

New Testament

40. Matthew
    A. Herod, King of Judea had great love for Jesus.
    B. Jesus asked Matthew to "Follow me."
    C. Jesus' death was not predicted by him.
    D. Peter denied Jesus four times.
    E. At the death of Jesus darkness covered the earth from the sixth to the eleventh hour.

41. Mark
    A. Jesus never walked on water.
    B. Jesus fed fifteen thousand people.
    C. To be great is to be last and servant of all.
    D. The poor widow gave a portion of her wealth into the temple treasury.

42. Luke
    A. Jesus was tempted by the devil for fifty days in the desert.
    B. The wind and water obeyed Jesus.
    C. The rich fool wanted to share all he had with the poor.

D. It is easier for the rich to enter heaven than a camel to get through the eye of a needle.

43. John
    A. The Samaritan woman was not from Samaria.
    B. Whoever follows Jesus will not walk in darkness.
    C. Barabbas took part in a rebellion as a robber.
    D. Thomas believed Jesus appeared to his disciples.

44. Acts
    A. All believers shared everything they had.
    B. Matthias replaced Judas as an apostle.
    C. Paul was a Jew from Tarsus.
    D. Handkerchiefs and aprons that touched Paul were used to heal the sick.
    E. Paul said, "Silver or gold I do not have."

45. Romans
    A. Paul went to Jerusalem to serve the saints.
    B. Sin entered the world through man.
    C. Very rarely will anyone die for a righteous man.

46. I Corinthians
   A. Paul was an apostle of man by the
       will of God.
   B. The wicked will not inherit the
       Kingdom of God.
   C. There are different kinds of gifts but
       one spirit.

47. II Corinthians
   A. Those who sow sparingly will reap
       sparingly.
   B. God reconciled man through Christ.
   C. Do not be yoked together with
       unbelievers.

48. Galatians
   A. A brother caught in sin should not
       be restored by the brothers.
   B. Sons of God come through faith in
       Christ Jesus.
   C. Christ gave himself for our sins.
   D. A sinful nature does not desire what
       is contrary to the spirit.

49. Ephesians
   A. Slaves should disobey their earthly
       masters and show no respect or fear.
   B. Paul did not consider himself a
       prisoner of Christ.
   C. A husband ought to love his wife as
       Christ loved the church.
   D. Children obey your parents in the
       Lord for this is right.

50. Philippians
    A. Paul said "watch out for those dogs,
        these men who do evil.
    B. Paul learned to be content in some
        situations.
    C. Paul was in chains for Christ.
    D. One should not look to his interest,
        but the interest of others.

51. Colossians
    A. Masters should not provide what is
        right for their slaves.
    B. Epaphras was a servant of Christ
        Jesus.
    C. Christ is the image of the invisible
        God.
    D. Paul was an apostle by the will of
        God.

52. I Thessalonians
    A. Christians should not try to live in
        peace with each other.
    B. Paul did not write a letter to the
        church in Thessalonica.
    C. The day of the Lord will come like a
        thief in the night.
    D. One is not saved through the
        sanctifying of the Holy Spirit.

53. II Thessalonians
    A. Paul, Silas, and Timothy were never
        friends.

B. Paul urged the brothers to pray for
   the message of God to spread.
C. The lawless will not perish because
   they do not love the truth.
D. God's judgment is not right.

54. I Timothy
   A. Paul charged Timothy to pursue
      righteousness.
   B. A little wine may be used for illness.
   C. The rich should not put their hope in
      wealth.
   D. Timothy was a true son in the faith
      to Paul.

55. II Timothy
   A. Paul did not request Timothy to
      bring Mark to Rome to see him.
   B. Paul stated, "I have fought the good
      fight, finished the course, finished
      the race and kept the faith."
   C. Paul to Timothy "Endure hardship
      like a good soldier."

56. Titus
   A. People should not be subject and
      obedient to rulers and authorities.
   B. People should slander one another.
   C. Young men should not have self-
      control.
   D. Titus was a true son in the faith to
      Paul.

57. Philemon
    A. Philemon has only one chapter.
    B. Onesimus was a slave of Philemon.
    C. Epaphras was a fellow prisoner in
       Christ with Paul.
    D. Onesimus aided Paul while he was
       in chains in Rome.

58. Hebrews
    A. One should not make every effort to
       live at peace with all men.
    B. Jesus did not taste death for
       everyone.
    C. Abraham gave Melchizedek a tenth
       of everything he had from the defeat
       of kings.
    D. Faith is being sure of what we hope
       for and certain of what we do not
       see.

59. James
    A. Bits are placed in the mouth of a
       horse to make him obey.
    B. Wisdom from heaven is not pure.
    C. Do not pray when trouble comes.
    D. Everyone should be quick to listen
       and slow to speak.

60. I Peter
    A. One should get rid of some deceit,
       envy, and slander.
    B. To be insulted because of the name
       of Christ is a blessing.

C. Love one another with sincere love
   from the heart.
D. Love does not cover a multitude of
   sins.

61. II Peter
    A. The Lord knows how to rescue godly
       men from trials.
    B. Prophecy had its origin in the will of
       man.
    C. The day of the Lord will come like a
       thief.
    D. With the Lord, a day is like a
       thousand years and a thousand years
       like a day.

62. I John
    A. Jesus Christ did not come in the flesh
       of God.
    B. Jesus Christ is the atoning sacrifice
       for our sins.
    C. God is light and in Him, there is no
       darkness.
    D. No one has ever seen God.

63. II John
    A. II John has two chapters.
    B. Christians should love one another.
    C. Deceivers acknowledge Jesus Christ.
    D. Christians should not separate
       themselves from false believers.

64. III John
    A. Paul addresses III John to Diotrephes
    B. "Imitate what is good" is given by
        John to Gaius.
    C. II John has three chapters.
    D. John thanked Gaius for his help with
        the church.

65. Jude
    A. Those who have been called are kept
        by Jesus Christ and love by the
        Father.
    B. The Lord delivered His people out of
        Egypt.
    C. Verses 23 and 24 of Jude are
        doxologies.

66. Revelation
    A. The church of Laodicea was
        lukewarm.
    B. John addressed seven churches in
        Asia.
    C. Jesus said "He is the bright and
        morning star.
    D. God said "He is Alpha and Omega.
    E. Book 66 closes with "The grace of the
        Lord Jesus be with God's people.
        Amen." (New International Bible)

Answers 40-66

40. Matthew
    B — Matthew 9:9

41. Mark
    C — Mark 9:35

42. Luke
    B — Luke 8:25

43. John
    B — John 8:12
    C — John 18:40

44. Acts
    A — Acts 4:32
    B — Acts 1:23-26
    C — Acts 21:39
    D — Acts 19:11
    E — Acts 3:6

45. Romans
    A — Romans 15:25
    B — Romans 5:12
    C — Romans 5:7

46. I Corinthians
    A — I Corinthians 6:9
    B — I Corinthians 12:4

47. II Corinthians
    A — II Corinthians 9:6

B — II Corinthians 5:17-18
C — II Corinthians 6:14

48. Galatians
B — Galatians 3:26
C — Galatians 1:3-4

49. Ephesians
— Ephesians 5:25
— Ephesians 6:1

50. Philippians
A — Philippians 3:2
C — Philippians 1:13
D — Philippians 2:4

51. Colossians
B — Colossians 4:12
C — Colossians 1:15
D — Colossians 1:1

52. I Thessalonians
C — I Thessalonians 5:2

53. II Thessalonians
B — II Thessalonians 3:1

54. I Timothy
A — I Timothy 6:11
B — I Timothy 5:23
C — I Timothy 6:17
D — I Timothy 1:2

55. II Timothy
B — II Timothy 4:7
C — II Timothy 2:3

56. Titus
        D — Titus 1:4

57. Philemon
        A — Philemon 1 - True
        B — Philemon 1:16
        C — Philemon 1:1 and Philemon 23
        D — Philemon 1:11

58. Hebrews
        C — Hebrews 7:2
        D — Hebrews 11:1

59. James
        A — James 3:3
        B — James 1:19

60. I Peter
        B — I Peter 4:14
        C — I Peter 1:22

61. II Peter
        A — II Peter 2:9
        C — II Peter 3:10
        D — II Peter 3:8

62. I John
        B — I John 2:1
        D — I John 4:12

63. II John
        B — II John 1:5

64. III John
        B — III John 1:11
        D — III John 3-5

65. Jude
> A — Jude 1:1
> B — Jude 1:5
> C — Jude 1:24 (Doxology) and Jude 1:25 (Doxology)

66. Revelations
> A — Revelations 3:14-16
> B — Revelations 1:4
> C — Revelations 22:16
> D — Revelations 1:8 and Revelations 22:13
> E — Revelations 22:21

Author

The author, Dr. Bernard Kent, Jr., is the father of three daughters and one son. That also includes two Godchildren, ten grandchildren, and three great-grandchildren that keep him active as a grandparent.

This book was written during the Coronavirus pandemic that affected the gathering of families in churches, schools, and many other social events. Much time is given for families to be together and enjoy one another. What better way than to become more familiar with each other. As an aide to families not being together, a phone call can lift spirits and never forget to pray for one another.

Dr. Kent resides in Savannah, Georgia, and attends the Savannah Church of God. He spends time reading, saltwater fishing, and gardening. Several books written by him include *"Forgiveness: A Process not an Act.," "Compliment with Encouragement," "Twenty-Seven Bible Crosswords,"* and *"Thirty-Nine Bible Crosswords."*